ESSENTIAL LIFE HACKS FOR KIDS AGE 8

BY TAYLOR FINN

Join our mailing list to be notified of new products!

Copyright © 2022 by Scholastic Arte Press
All rights reserved. This book or any portion thereof
may not be reproduced or used in any manner whatsoever
without the express written permission of the publisher
except for the use of brief quotations in a book review.
Printed in the United States of America
First Printing, 2022
Scholastic Arte Press
www.scholasticartepress.com

Table Of Contents

01 Hair Care Chronicles

02 Bed-Making Mastery

03 Morning Maestros

04 My Space, Your Space

05 The Friendship Symphony

06 The First Aid Adventures

07 Kitchen Capers

08 Food Detectives

09 Homework Heroes

10 Room Rangers

11 Typing Titans

12 Hobbies Galore

Hair Care Chronicles

In the Hair Care Kingdom, a magical land, Where locks are treated with a gentle hand. Shampoo symphony, a bubbly delight, Transforming your hair, oh, what a sight! Rinse rhapsody, a water dance so sweet, A rain shower melody, making hair neat. Conditioner concerto, a silky potion's kiss, Adding softness and shine, pure bliss. Detangling duet, a gentle, flowing song, Through the locks, where harmony belongs. Towel waltz in the grand ballroom, Patting dry gently, like a soft plume. Brushing ballad, a symphony of shine, Magical strokes, in a rhythm so divine. Hair, a crown of distinction and grace, Aroyal journey, every strand in its place. So, young explorers, heed this decree, Treat your locks with love, set them free. In the Hair Care Kingdom, you're the queen or king. A crown of shining tresses, let your royal hair sing!

Hello, young explorers of the Hair Care Kingdom! Today, we embark on an exciting journey into the world of hair washing and brushing. Imagine your hair as a crown waiting to shine with brilliance and strength! In this section, we'll delve into the art of keeping our locks clean, healthy, and oh-so-sparkly.

The Hair Care Adventure

The Shampoo Symphony:

Begin your Hair Care adventure with a burst of the shampoo symphony. Imagine the shampoo as a magical elixir, ready to transform your hair into a cascade of freshness. Massage the shampoo gently into your scalp, creating a bubbly masterpiece.

The Rinse Rhapsody:

Rinse away the shampoo with a melody of water droplets. Picture the water cleansing your hair like a refreshing rain shower. Ensure every bubble is gone, leaving your hair feeling rejuvenated and light.

The Conditioner Concerto:

Introduce the conditioner as the magical overture to softness and shine. Apply the conditioner and let it work its magic while you daydream of enchanted realms.

The Hair Care Adventure

The Detangling Duet:

After rinsing out the conditioner, it's time for the detangling duet. Use a wide-toothed comb to gently detangle your locks, starting from the tips and working your way up. Think of it as a harmonious duet between your hair and the comb.

The Towel Waltz:

Wrap your hair in a soft towel like a cozy dance partner. Picture yourself in the grand ballroom of the Hair Care Castle, where every step ensures your hair's royal treatment. Pat your hair dry gently, avoiding any vigorous rubbing.

The Brushing Ballad:

Once your hair is mostly dry, commence the brushing ballad. Hold your magical brush and gently glide through your locks. Picture each stroke as a note in a musical score, creating a symphony of shine fit for a Hair Care Queen or King.

The Secrets of Lustrous Locks

Treat your hair like royalty, for it is your crown of distinction. Regular care ensures your hair remains strong, healthy, and fit for a king or queen.

Patience is the Key:

Hair care requires patience and gentle care. Just like a garden needs time to blossom, your hair needs consistent love and attention.

Healthy Habits Last a Lifetime:

Building healthy hair care habits now will benefit you for a lifetime. Imagine your hair as a loyal companion that grows and flourishes with the right care.

Every Lock Tells a Story:

Your hair tells a story of your adventures, just like chapters in a book. Embrace the uniqueness of your locks' tales, and let them shine with every twist and turn.

Benefits of Hair Washing and Brushing

Strength and Growth:

Regular hair washing and brushing stimulate the scalp, promoting strong and healthy hair growth. It's like giving your hair the nutrients it needs to grow and flourish.

Tangle-Free Tresses:

Brushing helps prevent tangles and knots, making your hair easier to manage. It's like clearing a smooth path through the Hair Care Kingdom, ensuring your royal locks remain hassle-free.

Self-Care Ritual:

Hair care becomes a delightful self-care ritual. Imagine it as a royal ceremony where you pamper yourself and treat your hair with the utmost respect and kindness. of shining tresses, let your royal hair sing!

Congratulations, young explorers of the Hair Care Kingdom! You've now become custodians of sparkling tresses, ready to embark on countless royal adventures. So, embrace the magic of caring for your locks, dance with your brush, and let the symphony of shine continue to resonate in your enchanted Hair Care Kingdom!

Bed-Making Mastery

Hello, young bed-makers and adventurers! Today, we embark on a bedtime journey into the magical world of making your bed. Imagine your bed as a cozy castle waiting for your return each night! In this section, we'll explore the art of making your bed, turning it into a fortress of comfort and dreams.

The Bed-Making Quest

The Blanket Shake:

Begin your bedtime adventure with a magical blanket shake. Hold the corners of your blanket and give it a gentle shake, like a fairy sprinkling sleep dust. This helps spread the magic evenly across your bed.

The Stuffed Animal Parade:

If you have stuffed animals, let them join the bedtime parade. Arrange them neatly at the head of your bed, like loyal guardians watching over your dreams. They're your cuddly companions on this sleep-filled journey.

The Bookshelf Shuffle:

If you have a bedside bookshelf, organize it like a library of adventures. Line up your favorite bedtime stories, ready to transport you to faraway lands before you drift off to sleep.

The Secrets of Cozy Beds

A Made Bed Feels Like a Hug:

Making your bed is like giving it a warm, comforting hug. When you return after a busy day, your bed will be there, inviting you to relax and unwind.

Creativity in Bed-Making:

Bed-making is a chance to express your creativity. Imagine your bed as a canvas, and you're the artist arranging the elements to create a masterpiece of comfort.

Creativity in Bed-Making:

Bed-making is a chance to express your creativity. Imagine your bed as a canvas, and you're the artist arranging the elements to create a masterpiece of comfort.

The Importance of Order:

Making your bed helps create order in your bedroom. It's like organizing your magical kingdom, ensuring everything is in its place for a peaceful night's sleep.

A Made Bed Sets the Mood:

A neatly made bed sets the mood for bedtime adventures. It's like a welcoming stage where dreams take center stage, and you're the star of the show.

The Bedtime Brigade

Once upon a moonlit night in Sleepyville, lived a young adventurer named Alex. Alex loved bedtime adventures and dreamt of turning the ordinary act of making a bed into a grand quest.

One evening, as the stars twinkled overhead, Alex gathered the Blanket of Dreams and gave it a gentle shake. The stars on the blanket sparkled, as if whispering secrets of faraway galaxies. Next, Alex fluffed the pillows, imagining them as friendly clouds eager to cradle sweet dreams.

The tuck-in tornado came next. With a swish and a swoosh, Alex tucked in the sides of the blanket, creating a fortress of coziness. It was a magical barrier that kept out the bedtime monsters and invited only the sweetest of dreams.

As Alex surveyed the bed, the stuffed animals came to life. They lined up at the head of the bed, forming the Bedtime Brigade—a loyal team of guardians ready to protect Alex's dreams. Each stuffed animal had a role, from the brave teddy bear to the wise owl.

The bookshelf shuffle completed the bedtime adventure. Alex organized the bedside bookshelf like a library of enchanted tales. As Alex drifted off to sleep, the bedtime stories whispered promises of exciting journeys and mystical realms.

From that night on, Alex's bedtime routine became a grand quest, and Sleepyville buzzed with tales of the brave adventurer who turned bedtime into a magical adventure.

Hooray, young bed-makers and adventurers! You've now embarked on the bedtime journey of making your bed, turning it into a fortress of comfort and dreams. So, shake those blankets, fluff those pillows, and let the bedtime adventure begin each night in your magical castle of coziness! Sweet dreams, brave adventurers!

Morning Maestros

Good morning, young explorers! Today, we are diving into the fascinating world of time management for your morning routine. Imagine your mornings as a grand adventure waiting to unfold! In this section, we'll unravel the secrets of managing your time efficiently to ensure a fantastic start to each day.

The Morning Adventure Map

The Nighttime Blueprint:

Begin your morning adventure the night before. Lay out your clothes, pack your backpack, and make a list of things to do. It's like creating a nighttime blueprint for the exciting journey ahead.

The Wake-Up Wiggle:

When the morning sun peeks through your window, give yourself a wake-up wiggle. Stretch your arms and legs like a playful explorer, preparing your body for the adventures that await.

The Morning Adventure Map

The Pajama Race:

Turn getting dressed into a fun pajama race. Challenge yourself to see how quickly you can change into your daytime outfit. It's like a friendly competition with the ticking clock.

The Breakfast Bonanza:

Enjoy a breakfast bonanza with a nutritious meal. Picture your breakfast as the fuel that powers your morning adventure. Choose foods that energize you, like a superhero's breakfast.

The Brushing Blitz:

Turn teeth brushing into a brushing blitz. Imagine your toothbrush as a magical wand, protecting your teeth from sugar monsters. Brush with enthusiasm, ensuring your smile sparkles like a treasure.

The Backpack Checkpoint:

Before you dash out the door, perform a backpack checkpoint. Make sure you have everything you need for the day's quests—homework, lunch, and any tools for your learning adventures.

The Secrets of Morning Mastery

Time Is Your Ally:

Time is like a trusty sidekick on your morning adventure. Manage it wisely, and it will help you conquer each task with ease.

Every Second Counts:

Treasure every second of your morning routine. Imagine each second as a magical coin that adds to your adventure fund. The more coins you collect, the more successful your morning quest will be.

Stay Positive, Stay Productive:

A positive mindset is your morning compass. Stay positive, and your morning adventure will unfold smoothly. Positive thoughts are like magical keys that unlock a world of possibilities.

Adventure Awaits Every Morning:

Treat each morning as a new adventure waiting to be explored. Whether it's a quest for knowledge at school or a playtime adventure with friends, every morning holds exciting possibilities.

The Quest for the Golden Homework

Once upon a bright and early morning in Adventureville, lived a young explorer named Emma. Emma loved embarking on exciting quests, but one morning, the Golden Homework had vanished!

With a determined spirit, Emma followed the Morning Adventure Map. The nighttime blueprint guided her to pack her backpack with all the necessary tools for the day's quest. Emma imagined her backpack as a treasure chest ready to hold the Golden Homework once found.

As Emma embarked on the pajama race, she raced against the ticking clock. In record time, she transformed into her daytime explorer outfit, ready for the day's adventure. The wake-up wiggle added a sprinkle of energy, setting the tone for a positive morning quest.

The Quest for the Golden Homework

The breakfast bonanza fueled Emma's body with energy for the journey ahead. She imagined each bite as a power-up for her explorer skills. The brushing blitz turned teeth brushing into a magical ritual, ensuring her smile sparkled like the Golden Homework she sought.

At the backpack checkpoint, Emma discovered the Golden Homework hiding behind her math book. With a triumphant grin, she realized that managing her time wisely had led her to a successful morning quest.

From that day on, Emma continued her morning adventures, armed with the knowledge that time management was the key to unlocking the treasures of each day.

Congratulations, young explorers! You've now unlocked the secrets of time management for your morning routine. With the Morning Adventure Map, you can navigate your mornings with enthusiasm and efficiency. So, wake up with a wiggle, conquer the pajama race, and let each morning unfold as a fantastic adventure waiting to be explored! Happy questing!

My Space, Your Space Harmony

Greetings, young adventurers! Today, we embark on a special mission into the galaxy of personal space. Imagine personal space as a magical force field that each explorer possesses. In this section, we'll discover the art of respecting personal space—a key skill for harmonious adventures with fellow explorers.

The Space Explorer Code

The Invisible Hula Hoop:

Envision an invisible hula hoop around your body—this is your personal space bubble. When talking or playing, keep a comfortable distance, just like twirling an imaginary hula hoop. It ensures everyone has their own magical space.

The Permission Parley:

Before entering someone else's personal space, engage in a permission parley. Imagine asking, "May I join your space adventure?" Seeking permission shows respect for others' boundaries and ensures everyone feels comfortable.

The Listening Galaxy:

When someone is sharing their thoughts or feelings, enter the listening galaxy. Picture yourself in a spaceship, tuning into their transmission. Maintain a respectful distance and give them the space to express themselves.

The Friendly Orbit:

During group activities, maintain a friendly orbit. Imagine each explorer as a planet, and personal space as the orbits around them. Find your comfortable orbit, ensuring a harmonious and respectful coexistence.

The Body Language Decoder:

Learn the art of the body language decoder. Observe the signals others give—like crossed arms or stepping back. These signs indicate their comfort level in the personal space galaxy. Adjust your position accordingly.

The Galaxy's Rules and Wonders

Everyone Has a Space Galaxy:

Recognize that every explorer has their own unique space galaxy. Respecting personal space means acknowledging and valuing the boundaries of others, just as you cherish your own.

Boundaries Are Like Constellations:

Think of personal boundaries as constellations in the galaxy. Each boundary creates a unique pattern, contributing to the beauty and diversity of the personal space universe.

Comfort is the Guiding Star:

The guiding star in the personal space galaxy is comfort. Ensure that everyone feels comfortable in their own space, allowing for a joyful and cooperative journey through the universe of interactions.

Sharing Space is an Adventure:

Collaborating and sharing space can be an exciting adventure. Imagine it as a cosmic dance where explorers move harmoniously, respecting each other's orbits and creating a magical symphony.

The Galactic Gathering

Once upon a time in the Cosmos Camp, a group of young adventurers gathered for a cosmic celebration. Each explorer had their own unique space galaxy, filled with dreams and wonders. As the Galactic Gathering began, the adventurers engaged in the invisible hula hoop dance. They twirled their imaginary hoops, ensuring a comfortable distance between them. The permission parley became their universal language, with each explorer seeking consent before entering another's space.

During the storytelling session, the adventurers entered the listening galaxy. They formed a circle, maintaining a respectful orbit around the storyteller. The atmosphere was filled with curiosity and wonder as each adventurer shared their tales from the far reaches of their personal space.

Throughout the day, the friendly orbit guided the adventurers. During group activities, they found their harmonious orbits, respecting the boundaries of their fellow explorers. The body language decoder played a crucial role, helping them navigate the vastness of the personal space galaxy.

As the Galactic Gathering came to an end, the young adventurers reflected on the beauty of sharing space. They realized that by respecting each other's personal space, they had created a cosmic harmony that made their adventures even more delightful.

Congratulations, young adventurers! You've now completed your mission in the galaxy of personal space. By mastering the Space Explorer Code and understanding the wonders of the personal space universe, you can navigate social interactions with grace and respect. So, twirl your invisible hula hoop, seek permission with the parley, and let the magic of personal space make your adventures even more enchanting! Safe travels in the cosmic expanse of friendships!

The Friendship Symphony

In the land of friendship, where laughter resides, Sometimes conflicts arise, like ocean tides. But fear not, dear friends, for a funny rhyme, Will guide us through, it's resolution time! When notes go flat and tempers flare, Take a deep breath, let's clear the air. The calming cadence, a melody so sweet, Helps us find our harmony and regain our seat. Now, join the empathy ensemble, let's take a stroll, In our friend's shoes, understand their soul. Empathy's the bridge, connecting our hearts, In the friendship symphony, where healing starts. Communication concerto, let words take flight, Express your feelings, make everything right. "I feel" statements, like lyrics so clear, Compose the melody that all can hear. The solution serenade, a collaborative song, Where both friends play, nothing goes wrong. Together we brainstorm, a harmonious quest, Finding solutions, we truly are the best. And now, forgiveness fanfare, a trumpet so grand, Playing a melody across the friendship land. Forgive and forget, let's move ahead, In the friendship symphony, where joy is spread. So here's to laughter, and to making amends, To resolving conflicts, and making new friends. In the comedy of friendship, where we all play a part, Let's keep the harmony alive, it warms the heart!

The Harmony Composer's Toolkit

The Calming Cadence:
When conflicts arise, start with the calming cadence. Take a deep breath and count to three, just like a gentle melody. This helps you find your inner harmony before addressing the discord.

The Empathy Ensemble:

Join the empathy ensemble by putting yourself in your friend's shoes. Imagine their feelings and thoughts as a melody you want to understand. Empathy is the magical bridge that connects hearts and fosters understanding.

The Communication Concerto:

Engage in the communication concerto by expressing your feelings with words. Use "I feel" statements to share your emotions, just like crafting a heartfelt lyric. Honest communication is the key to resolving conflicts and keeping the friendship melody alive.

The Harmony Composer's Toolkit

The Solution Serenade:

Collaborate on the solution serenade. Imagine brainstorming together as composing a melody that harmonizes both your needs. Finding a solution that works for both friends is the sweetest note in the friendship symphony.

The Forgiveness Fanfare:

Conclude the conflict resolution with the forgiveness fanfare. Picture forgiveness as a triumphant trumpet that plays a melody of healing. Forgiving and moving forward is the grand finale that restores the friendship symphony.

The Musical Rules of Friendship

Friendship Is a Symphony:

Recognize that friendship is like a beautiful symphony, with each friend playing a unique instrument. Conflicts are moments when the melody may falter, but with effort, the harmony can be restored.

Empathy Is the Harmony Glue:

Understand that empathy is the glue that holds the friendship harmony together. When conflicts arise, empathizing with your friend's feelings creates a connection that transcends discord.

Communication Is the Conductor:

Acknowledge that communication is the conductor of the friendship orchestra. Expressing your feelings and listening to your friend's thoughts ensures that the melody stays melodious.

Solutions Create Sweet Melodies:

Appreciate that finding solutions together creates sweet melodies in the friendship symphony. Collaborating on resolutions brings harmony back to the relationship and strengthens the bond.

Bravo, young harmony seekers! You've now explored the musical art of resolving conflicts with friends. Remember, the friendship symphony is a beautiful composition that sometimes encounters a discordant note. With the Harmony Composer's Toolkit and the Musical Rules of Friendship, you have the power to restore the melody and keep the friendship symphony playing sweet tunes. So, embrace the magic of resolving conflicts, and let the harmony of friendship continue to resonate in your hearts!

The First Aid Adventures

Hello, young heroes! Today, we embark on an exciting adventure into the world of basic first aid. Imagine yourself as a superhero equipped with the skills to help others in need. In this section, we'll explore the basics of first aid, focusing on a fundamental skill: applying a band-aid.

The Heroic Band-Aid Application Quest

The Calm and Collected Stance:

When you or a friend gets a minor cut or scrape, channel your inner hero and assume a calm and collected stance. Take a deep breath, just like a superhero preparing for a mission. A composed mind is your greatest superpower.

The Washing Waterfall:

Begin the heroic band-aid application quest with the washing waterfall. Clean the cut or scrape with mild soap and water, imagining the water as a cleansing force that washes away any germs or dirt.

The Drying Wind Gust:

Once the area is clean, use a gentle patting motion to dry it with a clean cloth. Picture a drying wind gust that prepares the battleground for the band-aid.

The Magical Band-Aid Unveiling:

Now, unveil the magical band-aid from its protective covering. Imagine it as a shield that will protect the wounded area and promote healing. Peel it gently, unveiling the superhero cape for your cut or scrape.

The Precise Placement Artistry:

With precision and care, place the band-aid over the cut or scrape. Picture yourself as a skilled artist, ensuring that the band-aid covers the wounded area completely. Smooth out any wrinkles, creating a comfortable and protective barrier.

The Gentle Press of Healing:

Press down gently on the band-aid, activating its healing powers. Imagine your touch as a magical force that encourages the band-aid to adhere to the skin. This step ensures the band-aid stays in place during your heroic adventures.

The Secrets of Heroic First Aid

Cuts and Scrapes Happen to Everyone:

Understand that cuts and scrapes are part of life's adventures. Even heroes get minor injuries, but with the power of first aid, you can overcome them.

Cleanliness is the Shield:

Know that cleanliness is your shield against infection. Washing the wounded area with soap and water is like preparing the battleground for a victorious battle against germs.

Band-Aids are Heroic Helpers:

Acknowledge that band-aids are your heroic helpers. They protect the wounded area, allowing it to heal faster and with less discomfort. Treat band-aids as the capes that superheroes wear to shield them from harm.

First Aid is a Superpower:

Realize that knowing first aid is a superpower. With these skills, you become a hero capable of helping others and yourself in times of need. Embrace the responsibility that comes with this extraordinary ability.

The Brave Band-Aid Brigade

Once upon a sunny day in Adventureland, a group of young heroes, known as the Brave Band-Aid Brigade, set out on a quest to explore the enchanted forest. As they ventured deeper into the woods, their path became treacherous, and one of the heroes, Lily, tripped over a protruding tree root.

Lily emerged with a small scrape on her knee, a battle wound from the forest floor. The Brave Band-Aid Brigade gathered around, ready to deploy their heroic first aid skills. The leader, Alex, assumed a calm and collected stance, encouraging Lily to take deep breaths.

As Lily bravely faced the washing waterfall, the youngest member, Mia, imagined the water cleansing the wounded area like a magical stream. Lily's knee, now washed, awaited the drying wind gust. The heroes used their cloths, gently patting the area dry, envisioning the wind preparing the battleground for the band-aid.

The magical band-aid was unveiled by Oliver, the band-aid specialist. It was a superhero cape with adhesive powers ready to protect Lily's knee. With precise placement artistry, the band-aid was applied, covering the scrape completely. Lily felt the gentle press of healing as Mia pressed down, activating the band-aid's magical force.

The Brave Band-Aid Brigade celebrated their victory, knowing that Lily's knee was now shielded and on its way to healing. They continued their adventure, now more confident in their first aid superpowers, ready to face any challenges the enchanted forest might throw their way.

Congratulations, young heroes! You've completed your first aid adventure and mastered the heroic skill of applying a band-aid. Remember, first aid is a superpower that empowers you to be a hero for yourself and others. So, embrace the responsibility, keep your superhero capes (band-aids) at the ready, and continue your adventures with the confidence of a true hero!

Kitchen Capers: Young Chefs Unleashed

Hello, little culinary wizards! Today, we embark on a delightful adventure into the world of basic cooking. Imagine your kitchen as a magical laboratory where you can create delicious wonders. In this section, we'll explore the basics of cooking, emphasizing safety and fun for young chefs like you.

The Culinary Wizardry Basics

The Apron Armor:

Before entering the kitchen, don your apron armor. This magical garment shields your clothes from spills and stains, ensuring you stay neat and tidy throughout your cooking adventure.

The Clean Hands Charm:

Start with the clean hands charm. Wash your hands thoroughly with soap and water, imagining it as a magical spell that banishes any germs. Clean hands are the foundation of a successful culinary journey.

The Ingredient Gathering Spell:

Cast the ingredient gathering spell before you begin. Collect all the ingredients needed for your magical recipe, organizing them like spell components on your kitchen counter. This step ensures a smooth and organized cooking process.

The Utensil Enchantment:

Enchant your utensils with a quick rinse under running water. Picture the water as a magical potion that awakens your utensils for the culinary spellcasting ahead. Dry them with a wave of your wand (or a towel) before diving into the cooking cauldron.

The Supervised Stirring Spell:

For young chefs, the supervised stirring spell is crucial. When working near heat or using sharp tools, always have a grown-up wizard by your side to guide you through the cooking magic. Stir, whisk, and mix under their watchful eye, ensuring a safe and enjoyable experience.

The Secrets of Culinary Wizardry

Every Chef is a Wizard:

Understand that every chef, no matter how small, is a wizard in the kitchen. Cooking is a magical skill that allows you to create tasty potions and treats to share with friends and family.

Safety Spells Come First:

Know that safety spells come first in the kitchen. Always have a grown-up wizard present when using the stove, oven, or any sharp tools. Safety is the most important ingredient in the recipe for culinary success.

Mistakes Are Magical Lessons:

Embrace the idea that mistakes are magical lessons. If a sprinkle of flour goes astray or a drop of sauce escapes, see it as a part of the enchanting journey. Learn from these magical moments and continue your culinary adventure with a smile.

Share Your Culinary Creations:

Discover the joy of sharing your culinary creations. Whether it's a magical cookie spell or a potion of fruit salad, spreading the joy of your kitchen magic with others is a wonderful way to showcase your skills.

Magic Fruit Wand Recipe

Ingredients:
Assorted fruits (such as grapes, strawberries, and melon chunks)
Wooden skewers or popsicle sticks
Yogurt or honey for dipping

Instructions:

Wash and Prepare:
Wash your hands with the clean hands charm, then gather your assortment of fruits. Cut larger fruits into bite-sized pieces with the help of a grown-up wizard.

Skewer Magic:
Take a wooden skewer or popsicle stick and start skewering the fruit pieces. Imagine you're casting a spell, creating a magical wand with colorful fruits.

Dip in Delight:
Dip your fruit wand into yogurt or honey, turning it into a delicious magical potion. Picture the dip as the enchanting coating that adds a touch of sweetness to your creation.

Once your magic fruit wands are ready, enjoy the enchanting flavors of your culinary creation. Share them with friends and family, and bask in the magic of your first kitchen adventure.

Bravo, little culinary wizards! You've now embarked on the magical journey of basic cooking skills. Remember, every chef is a wizard in the kitchen, and safety spells come first. Whether you're stirring a cauldron of soup or creating magic fruit wands, let the joy of cooking fill your heart with enchantment. So, don your apron armor, gather your ingredients, and continue your culinary adventures with the spirit of a true kitchen wizard!

Food Detectives

Hello, young food detectives! Today, we embark on a thrilling adventure to become experts in identifying healthy and unhealthy foods. Imagine yourself as a savvy detective, equipped with the tools to make wise choices for your body. In this section, we'll explore the basics of distinguishing between foods that fuel your adventures and those that may not be as friendly to your health.

The Detective's Toolbox

The Colorful Clue Hunt:

Begin your detective work with the colorful clue hunt. Explore the vibrant world of fruits and vegetables. These colorful treasures are packed with essential nutrients and are often a sign of a healthy food choice. Picture each color as a clue leading you to a nutritional jackpot.

The Ingredient Investigation:

Conduct an ingredient investigation when examining packaged foods. Flip the package and read the ingredient list carefully. Healthy foods usually have simple and recognizable ingredients. If you encounter mysterious and unfamiliar words, it might be a clue that the food is not as wholesome.

The Sugar Sneak Detective:

Unmask hidden sugars with the sugar sneak detective technique. Check the nutrition label for the amount of added sugars. Healthy foods tend to be lower in added sugars, while unhealthy ones might have a sugary surprise. Picture yourself as a sugar detective, protecting your taste buds from sneaky sweet invaders.

The Portion Patrol:

Keep an eye on portion sizes with the portion patrol technique. Even healthy foods can be less beneficial if consumed in large quantities. Picture your plate as a treasure map, and allocate space wisely for a balanced and nutritious meal.

The Water Wisdom:

Quench your thirst with water wisdom. Make water your beverage of choice, as it hydrates your body without added sugars or calories. Imagine every sip as a refreshing gulp of pure detective fuel, keeping you sharp and focused.

The Secrets of Nutritional Sleuthing

Nutrients are the Detective's Allies:

Understand that nutrients are your allies in the detective's quest. Healthy foods are rich in vitamins, minerals, and other essential nutrients that fuel your body and mind. Learn to identify these nutritional superheroes for optimal health.

Whole Foods are Wholesome:

Know that whole foods are often the most wholesome choices. Fruits, vegetables, whole grains, and lean proteins are your trusted companions in the quest for healthy eating. These foods come straight from nature, offering a bounty of nutritional benefits.o make healthy choices.

Balance is the Detective's Code:

Embrace the detective's code of balance. No food is entirely off-limits, but maintaining a balance is crucial. Enjoy treats in moderation, and let the majority of your choices be guided by the colorful clues and nutritional allies.

Listen to Your Body's Signals:

Tune in to your body's signals as a detective listens for clues. Pay attention to feelings of hunger and fullness. Eating slowly and savoring each bite helps you connect with your body's natural cues, guiding you t

Congratulations, young food detectives! You've completed your crash course in identifying healthy vs. unhealthy foods. Remember, the colorful clues, ingredient investigations, sugar sneak detection, portion patrol, and water wisdom are your trusty tools in the detective's toolbox. As you continue your nutritional sleuthing, let the secrets of nutrient allies and whole foods guide you toward a healthy and happy life. So, put on your detective hat, grab your tools, and embark on the delicious adventure of making wise food choices!

Homework Heroes

Hello, young scholars! Today, we embark on an exciting journey to become Homework Heroes. Imagine yourself as a superhero with the power to keep track of assignments and conquer homework challenges. In this section, we'll explore the basics of staying organized and share some fun hacks to make homework time a breeze.

The Homework Hero's Toolkit

The Mighty Planner:
Equip yourself with the mighty planner, your most essential tool. Choose a colorful planner or notebook and make it your homework headquarters. Write down assignments, due dates, and any special notes from your teachers. Picture it as your secret weapon for staying on top of your homework game.

The Daily Check-In Ritual:

Develop the daily check-in ritual. Set aside a few minutes each day to review your planner. This ritual helps you stay aware of upcoming assignments, ensuring no homework challenge catches you by surprise. Imagine it as your superhero routine, keeping your mind sharp and ready for action.

The Super Reminder System:

Create a super reminder system for important dates. Use alarms, sticky notes, or even a friendly reminder from a grown-up hero to keep track of deadlines. Picture yourself as the commander of your reminder army, ensuring no assignment is left behind.

The Homework Habitat:

Design a special homework habitat. Choose a quiet and well-lit space for your homework adventures. Make it comfortable with your favorite supplies, snacks, and a splash of creativity. Picture this habitat as your secret lair, where you can focus and unleash your homework superpowers.

The Celebratory Sticker Chart:

Introduce the celebratory sticker chart as a motivational hack. Create a chart with spaces for each completed assignment. Every time you finish a task, reward yourself with a colorful sticker. Imagine the chart as a treasure map, leading you to victory and a sense of accomplishment.

The Wisdom of Homework Heroes

Homework is Your Ally, Not Your Foe:

Understand that homework is your ally, not your foe. It's an opportunity to practice and reinforce what you've learned in class. Embrace each assignment as a chance to showcase your growing knowledge and skills.

Organization is the Homework Hero's Shield:

Know that organization is the Homework Hero's shield. A well-kept planner and a tidy homework habitat are your secret weapons against chaos. Stay organized, and you'll navigate the homework landscape with ease.

Asking for Help is a Superpower:

Realize that asking for help is a superpower. If you encounter challenges or don't understand an assignment, don't hesitate to seek guidance from your teachers, classmates, or grown-up heroes.

Superheroes are never afraid to ask for assistance.

Effort is the Homework Hero's Badge:

Acknowledge that effort is the Homework Hero's badge of honor. Even if a task seems challenging, giving your best effort is a victory in itself. Celebrate your hard work and dedication as you conquer each assignment.

Homework Heroes Learn and Grow:

Embrace the wisdom that Homework Heroes learn and grow. Each assignment is a stepping stone in your educational journey. Embrace the lessons, celebrate your successes, and use any challenges as opportunities to become an even mightier Homework Hero.

4 Homework Hacks for Young Scholars

Color Code Your Subjects:

Assign a specific color to each subject in your planner. For example, use green for math, blue for English, and so on. This color-coded system makes it easy to visually identify assignments for each subject.

Create a Homework Playlist:

Make homework time more enjoyable by creating a special playlist. Choose music that helps you focus and makes the homework habitat a fun and motivating space. Your favorite tunes can turn even the toughest assignments into an exciting adventure.

Use Fun Stamps for Completed Tasks:

Add a touch of fun to your celebratory sticker chart by incorporating stamps. Choose stamps with playful designs or characters that make completing assignments even more rewarding. Stamp your chart after each task for a burst of joy.

Incorporate Brain Breaks:

Break up longer homework sessions with brain breaks. Take short breaks to stretch, snack, or do a quick activity you enjoy. Picture these breaks as your superhero power-ups, recharging your mind for the next homework challenge.

Room Rangers

Hello, young rangers! Today, we embark on a fantastic journey to become Room Rangers. Imagine your room as a magical kingdom waiting to be discovered and organized. In this section, we'll explore the art of cleaning your room, transforming it into a haven of order and imagination.

The Room Ranger's Adventure Guide

The Magical Sorting Hat:

Begin your Room Ranger adventure with the magical sorting hat. Imagine yourself as a wizard sorting magical objects into different piles. Create three piles: one for toys, one for clothes, and one for things that belong in other parts of the house.

The Enchanting Toy Tidying Spell:

Cast the enchanting toy tidying spell to organize your toys. Find a special place for each type of toy, whether it's a designated shelf, box, or basket. Picture yourself as a toy wizard, arranging your toys with care and creativity.

The Clothes Folding Quest:

Embark on the clothes folding quest to conquer the mountain of laundry. Fold your clothes neatly and place them in their rightful drawers or hangers.

Imagine each folded garment as a treasure, waiting to be discovered when you get dressed.

The Dusting and Wiping Expedition:

Launch the dusting and wiping expedition to banish dust and bring shine to your kingdom. Use a duster or a clean cloth to wipe surfaces like desks, shelves, and dressers. Picture yourself as a dust-busting hero, ensuring your room sparkles like a magical palace.

The Wisdom of Room Rangers

Your Room, Your Kingdom:

Understand that your room is your kingdom. Keeping it tidy is not just a chore but a way to create a space where your imagination can soar. A clean room is a canvas for adventures waiting to unfold.

Every Item Has a Home:

Know that every item in your room has a home. Toys, clothes, and treasures each have their special place. By giving them a home, you create order and make it easier to find things when you need them.

Cleaning Can Be Fun:

Embrace the wisdom that cleaning can be fun. Turn on your favorite music, create a cleaning playlist, or imagine that you're on a quest to organize a magical realm. Transforming cleaning into a game makes it an exciting adventure.

Teamwork Makes the Kingdom Shine:

Acknowledge that teamwork makes the kingdom shine. If you have siblings or friends, consider turning cleaning into a group adventure. You can work together, share ideas, and celebrate the joy of a sparkling kingdom.

The Quest for a Sparkling Kingdom

Once upon a time in the land of Adventureville, lived a young explorer named Megan. Megan's room was like a magical kingdom filled with treasures, toys, and tales waiting to be discovered. One sunny morning, Megan decided to embark on a quest to transform her room into a sparkling kingdom.

Armed with a magical sorting hat, Megan started by sorting her toys into different piles. She imagined herself as a toy wizard, creating a magical display on her shelves and organizing her stuffed animals into a cozy kingdom. The toys cheered, excited to have their own special places.

Next, Megan set out on the clothes folding quest. She folded her clothes neatly, imagining each piece as a royal garment ready for a grand adventure. As she placed them in their drawers, her clothes formed a colorful tapestry, bringing life to her kingdom.

The dusting and wiping expedition followed. Megan became a dust-busting hero, banishing dust bunnies and bringing shine to her kingdom's surfaces. She wiped away imaginary cobwebs, making room for new stories and magical moments.

Summoning the magical bin, Megan collected items that didn't belong in her room. She pictured the bin as a teleportation device, sending misplaced items to their proper places in the house. Her room felt lighter and more organized with every item finding its rightful home.

As Megan admired her sparkling kingdom, she realized that cleaning could be a fun and magical adventure. She turned on her favorite music and danced around her room, celebrating the joy of a tidy space. Megan's room had transformed into a haven of order and imagination, ready for new explorations and exciting quests.

Typing Titans

Hello, young wordsmiths! Today, we embark on an exciting journey to become Typing Titans. Imagine your keyboard as a magical portal to a world of words and stories. In this section, we'll explore the basics of developing keyboard typing skills, unlocking the power to express your thoughts and ideas with the speed and precision of a true wordsmith.

The Typing Titan's Adventure Map

The Home Row Haven:
Begin your Typing Titan adventure by discovering the Home Row Haven. Place your fingers on the middle row of keys, with your left hand on ASDF and your right hand on JKL;. Imagine the home row as your base camp, the starting point for all your typing quests.

The Finger Friends Technique:

Make friends with your fingers using the Finger Friends technique. Assign each finger a specific set of keys to control. Your index fingers handle the keys closest to them, and as you move outward, each finger controls a set of keys. Picture your fingers as a team of superheroes, working together to conquer the keyboard.

The Dance of Words:

Engage in the dance of words as you explore the keyboard. When typing a word, use the Finger Friends technique to press each key in a rhythmic and controlled manner. Imagine your fingers dancing across the keys, creating a beautiful symphony of words on the screen.

The Spacebar Shuttle Launch:

Master the spacebar shuttle launch for a smooth typing experience. After typing a word, use your right thumb to press the spacebar. Picture the spacebar as a shuttle launch, propelling your words forward into the vast expanse of your writing universe.

The Secrets of Typing Titans

Practice Makes Perfect:

Understand that practice makes perfect in the world of Typing Titans. Set aside time each day to practice your typing skills. Whether it's typing short sentences, your favorite words, or even a mini story, consistent practice will make you a keyboard maestro.

Eyes on the Screen, Not the Keys:

Know the importance of keeping your eyes on the screen, not the keys. Trust your Finger Friends to find the right keys, and let your eyes focus on the words taking shape. This skill helps you become a faster and more confident typist.

Patience is a Virtue:

Embrace the wisdom that patience is a virtue when learning to type. It's okay to make mistakes and hit the wrong keys; every Typing Titan started as a beginner. With time and practice, you'll develop the skills to type with speed and accuracy.

Three Tips for Young Typists

Use Typing Games:

Incorporate typing games into your practice routine. There are fun and interactive games designed to improve your typing skills while making learning feel like play. Challenge yourself with games that involve words, sentences, and even magical adventures.

Create Your Own Stories:

Spark your creativity by typing your own stories. Imagine yourself as a storyteller, weaving tales on the keyboard. This not only enhances your typing skills but also allows you to express your thoughts and ideas through the magic of words.

Celebrate Milestones:

Celebrate your typing milestones along the way. Whether it's typing a sentence without looking at the keys or completing a paragraph with fewer mistakes, every achievement is a step closer to becoming a Typing Titan. Treat yourself to a small celebration to mark your progress.

Congratulations, young Typing Titans! You've now embarked on a thrilling adventure to master the basics of keyboard typing. Remember the Home Row Haven, the Finger Friends technique, and the dance of words as you explore the keyboard. Practice consistently, keep your eyes on the screen, and be patient with yourself as you become a keyboard maestro.

Hobbies Galore

Hello, young explorers! Today, we embark on an exciting journey to discover the magic of hobbies. Imagine hobbies as enchanted portals to new worlds of creativity and fun. In this section, we'll explore the joy of exploring and learning new hobbies, unlocking the door to a realm of endless possibilities.

The Explorer's Treasure Map to Hobbies

The Curiosity Compass:

Start your hobby exploration with the curiosity compass. Let your interests guide you like a compass needle pointing north. What makes you curious? What activities make your heart dance with excitement? Use your curiosity as a compass to discover hobbies that align with your passions.

The Hobby Safari:

Embark on a hobby safari to explore different activities. Imagine yourself as an adventurer in the wild, encountering various hobbies like exotic creatures. Try out a bit of painting, experiment with science projects, or dive into the world of music.

The Playful Practice Routine:

Engage in a playful practice routine to hone your hobby skills. Set aside dedicated time each day or week to immerse yourself in your chosen activity. Practice not as a task but as a joyful playtime, where you explore, experiment, and let your creativity soar. Imagine every practice session as a step closer to mastering your hobby.

Five Cool Hobbies to Explore

Painting and Drawing:

Dive into the colorful world of painting and drawing. Grab your paintbrushes, colored pencils, or markers, and let your imagination flow onto paper or canvas. Create landscapes, characters, or abstract art that reflects your unique style.

Musical Adventures:

Embark on musical adventures by learning to play an instrument. Whether it's a guitar, keyboard, or even a ukulele, explore the magic of creating melodies. Imagine yourself as a musical maestro, composing tunes that resonate with your emotions.

Science Experiments:

Become a scientist on a mission with exciting science experiments. Gather materials for simple experiments and watch as chemical reactions, colorful creations, and fascinating discoveries unfold before your eyes. Picture yourself as a mad scientist exploring the wonders of the scientific world.

Gardening Magic:

Discover the magic of gardening by cultivating your own green oasis. Plant seeds, nurture plants, and watch as your garden blossoms. Imagine yourself as a nature wizard, bringing life to the soil and enjoying the beauty of blooming flowers or delicious homegrown vegetables.

Storytelling Adventures:

Embark on storytelling adventures by writing your own stories or creating comics. Let your creativity flow as you invent characters, craft exciting plots, and bring your tales to life. Imagine yourself as a wordsmith, weaving stories that transport readers to fantastical realms.

www.ingramcontent.com/pod-product-compliance
Lightning Source LLC
Chambersburg PA
CBHW042119100526
44587CB00025B/4122